WAYS TO DEVELOPING RESILIENCE AMONG STUDENTS

DR DHEERAJ MEHROTRA

Copyright © Dr Dheeraj Mehrotra
All Rights Reserved.

This book has been published with all efforts taken to make the material error-free after the consent of the author. However, the author and the publisher do not assume and hereby disclaim any liability to any party for any loss, damage, or disruption caused by errors or omissions, whether such errors or omissions result from negligence, accident, or any other cause.

While every effort has been made to avoid any mistake or omission, this publication is being sold on the condition and understanding that neither the author nor the publishers or printers would be liable in any manner to any person by reason of any mistake or omission in this publication or for any action taken or omitted to be taken or advice rendered or accepted on the basis of this work. For any defect in printing or binding the publishers will be liable only to replace the defective copy by another copy of this work then available.

Contents

Preface

The book "Ways to Developing Resilience Among Students" talks about building the students stronger to face and overcome any failure. It talks about how a student learns to handle hurdles. Building resilience in students begins in the classroom. It is the key to making young people more robust and more assertive. As we know, Resilience is an individual's capacity to cope with, adapt to, and recover from situations of adversity. Hence as a priority, it is housed as a practice to stay happy and informed as a part of mindfulness.

Strength means having the ability to overcome stressful, challenging and sometimes traumatic experiences in our lives. The book talks about similar gestures in action.

Happy Reading!

Dr Dheeraj Mehrotra

www.authordheerajmehrotra.com

ONE

DEVELOPING RESILIENCE AMONG STUDENTS

The ability to encounter and overcome adversity in ways that retain or enhance well-being is referred to as resilience. It includes characteristics such as grit, persistence, innovation, and determination. There are many different routes to achievement. In every available situation, students should be encouraged to look for chances to do something constructive. to be charitable, to make a positive contribution to one's society and to the greater good, and to help other people in some manner.

The following are the ways we can help our kids develop Resilience among our students.

By helping and encouraging them.

ϞϞϞ

Pay attention to your health.

ϞϞϞ

By balancing our work n situations.

ϞϞϞ

I am taking care of mental health.

ᐳᐳᐳ

I am keeping patient.

ᐳᐳᐳ

Pay attention to your health.

ᐳᐳᐳ

*You are focusing on your physical well-being
and mental well-being.*

ᐳᐳᐳ

Practice relaxation techniques.

ᗞᗞᗞ

Practice reframing threats as challenges.

ᗞᗞᗞ

Mind your mindset.

ᗞᗞᗞ

Get connected.

ৡৡৡ

Practice self-awareness.

ৡৡৡ

Watch your stress levels.

ৡৡৡ

It helps to improve ourselves.

ৡৡৡ

Keep up the positive and productive mindset.

ᑭᑭᑭ

Think positive.

ᑭᑭᑭ

You can't always control life-changing events,

but you can control how you respond to them.

ᑭᑭᑭ

Look after yourself.

ᕕᕕᕕ

Use your support network.

ᕕᕕᕕ

Work towards a goal.

ᕕᕕᕕ

Seek help.

ϿϿϿ

To be flexible.

ϿϿϿ

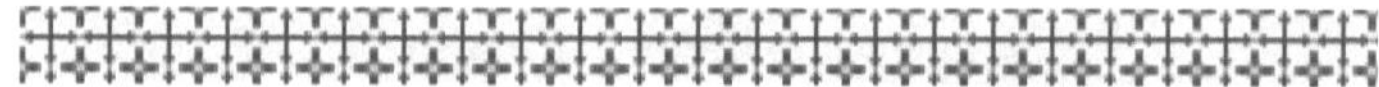

Focus on your physical well-being.

ϿϿϿ

By having a positive attitude.

ϿϿϿ

Practise and adapt to changes.

❧❧❧

Following a positive approach at work and a positive outlook in life, in turn, enables better problem-solving and helps to maintain motivation.

❧❧❧

Patience and hard work.

❧❧❧

Focus on my work

Authenticity. You know and hold onto your values, deploy your strengths, and have excellent emotional awareness and regulation. Purpose. Your work offers purpose and a sense of belonging, Adaptability—self-care, Support, Energy and Networks.

ϸϸϸ

By building up confidence and cooperation with others.

ϸϸϸ

Initiate the students for self-confidence.

ϸϸϸ

To identify our inner critic, practice mindfulness.

ϸϸϸ

Working on it.. sometimes it takes time.

ϸϸϸ

Think positive. You can't always control life-changing events, but you can control how you respond to them.

ϸϸϸ

Look after yourself.

ϸϸϸ

Use your support network.

ppp

Work towards a goal.

ppp

Seek help.

ppp

We are accepting challenges.

❦❦❦

Pay attention to your health.

❦❦❦

Focus on your physical well-being.

❦❦❦

Practice relaxation techniques.

❦❦❦

Practice reframing threats as challenges.

ᐅᐅᐅ

Mind your mindset.

ᐅᐅᐅ

Get connected.

ᐅᐅᐅ

Practice self-awareness.

ᐅᐅᐅ

Watch your stress levels.

ꕥꕥꕥ

Practice self-awareness

ꕥꕥꕥ

By handling situations positively.

ꕥꕥꕥ

Accepting is accepting challenges as a priority.

ᐇᐇᐇ

Teach students to become aware of when the feeling of negativity arises.

ᐇᐇᐇ

Resilience enables a positive approach to work.

ᐇᐇᐇ

Control emotions.

ᐇᐇᐇ

Resilience is a critical strategy that helps employees tackle stress, a competitive job market, workplace conflicts, and challenges. Improving resilience is essential because employees identify work as the number one stressor in their lives.

ÞÞÞ

Pay attention to your health.

ÞÞÞ

By being Patience

ÞÞÞ

Concentration

ÞÞÞ

Overcome challenges

ᔅᔅᔅ

In the daily teaching process.

ᔅᔅᔅ

*Paying attention to your health
focus on physical well being
practising relaxation techniques
watching stress levels.*

ᔅᔅᔅ

Experiential learning format, exposure to different situations of life

by facing all the difficulties with a smile.

ᐅᐅᐅ

Do exercise or anything you like during a break.

ᐅᐅᐅ

Always remain calm while teaching.

ᐅᐅᐅ

By maintaining emotional balance,

By having flexibility, not getting stressed, accepting n moving ahead

Perseverance,

Health, relaxation, mindset etc.,

Counselling.

❧❧❧

By helping the students by creating a supportive learning environment.

❧❧❧

Get connected

❧❧❧

Do work hard

ϷϷϷ

Focus on your physical well being

ϷϷϷ

Increase belongingness, develop problem-solving skills, and overcome the fear of failure.

ϷϷϷ

Resilience in the workplace can help people recover from challenging experiences. It can also assist their growth and development. Data from BetterUp members shows that those experiencing change also experience growth.

❧❧❧

By coping and gaining the confidence that I can do my best.

❧❧❧

thought meditation and a positive approach towards things happening...whatever happens -happens for our good..even though we might not be able to understand it at that time.

❧❧❧

Learn from our mistakes and failures.

❧❧❧

However, it's not just a reactive skill that switches on when a person faces challenges. It also enables a proactive approach to daily life.

ϷϷϷ

Being practical

ϷϷϷ

Setting an example

ϷϷϷ

This can be applied to employees' abilities to manage a demanding workload to frustration in a workplace setting.

ᗷᗷᗷ

Focus on physical well-being, practice relaxation techniques, mind your mindset and practice self-awareness

ᗷᗷᗷ

By flexible approach

ᗷᗷᗷ

Helping other students or contributing to the community helps develop new skills and instils a sense of purpose.

ᗷᗷᗷ

Treat problems as a learning process, celebrate success, and yes, you can do it.

ɣɣɣ

By guiding or counselling and practice flexibility etc.

ɣɣɣ

Focus on your physical well-being.

ɣɣɣ

Accept the facts, understand change is part of life, pursue a hobby, do things you like, talk to someone, share, learn to deal with emotions, and maintain a positive attitude towards life.

ϸϸϸ

Learning from mistakes and handling situations in a relaxed manner.

ϸϸϸ

Learning to relax, practice thought awareness, set personal goals, and build self-confidence.

ϸϸϸ

Rational thinking, flexibility, facing challenges s as they come, acceptance.

ϸϸϸ

.Keep on working even after failures.

ᕫᕫᕫ

Pay attention to your health

ᕫᕫᕫ

Focus on your physical well-being.

ᕫᕫᕫ

Practice relaxation techniques.

ᗵᗵᗵ

Practice reframing threats as challenges.

ᗵᗵᗵ

Mind your mindset.

ᗵᗵᗵ

Get connected.

ᗵᗵᗵ

Practice self-awareness.

༜༜༜

Watch your stress levels.

༜༜༜

With confidence, relaxed and calm nature and controlled actions.

༜༜༜

Perseverance and patience.

༜༜༜

We come across various problems in our life. They can be overcome by cultivating a joyful environment and being peaceful.

ϷϷϷ

Resilience is a critical strategy that helps employees tackle stress, a competitive job market, workplace conflicts, and challenges.

ϷϷϷ

Resilience means overcoming any kind of stress.

ϷϷϷ

1. Pay attention to your health
2. Focus on your physical well-being
3. Practice relaxation techniques
4. Practice reframing threats as challenges
5. Mind your mindset
6. Get connected
7. Practice self-awareness
8. Watch your stress levels

❦❦❦

Take things as they come, can overcome hardships, and develop confidence.

❦❦❦

By practising

❦❦❦

Watch the stress level of students and practice relaxation techniques.

ᏬᏬᏬ

Mindset, get connected by practising self-awareness

ᏬᏬᏬ

Creating a positive classroom environment and motivating everyone's participation in a classroom activity.

ᏬᏬᏬ

Pay attention to your health.

ᏬᏬᏬ

By self-awareness, minding the mindset, hitting back the problems

ᢒᢒᢒ

By encouraging students to ask questions self-awareness and practice self-awareness

ᢒᢒᢒ

Resilience is a critical strategy that helps employees tackle stress, a competitive job market, workplace conflicts, and challenges.

ᢒᢒᢒ

We can attain resilience at work through several ways, like taking a break from time to time, making a checklist before starting or restarting the job, learning from our bitter experiences and failure, stopping ourselves from getting distracted and affected by negative comments and always believing in ourselves being positively motivated to achieve success.

ϸϸϸ

With patience and understanding

ϸϸϸ

Health and well-being, mind our mindset, practice

ϸϸϸ

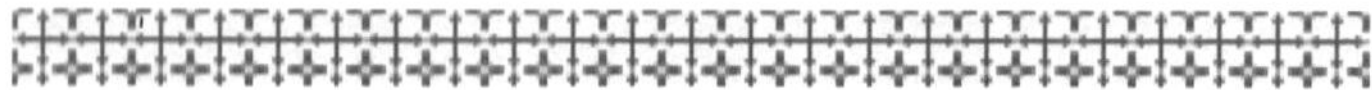

Exercise mindfulness

ↂↂↂ

*Compartmentalise your cognitive load
Take detachment breaks
Develop mental agility
Cultivate compassion*

ↂↂↂ

Think positive. You can't always control life-changing events, but you can control how you respond to them.

ↂↂↂ

By being confident, coping with situations, staying connected and contributing whatever is needed at work.

ↂↂↂ

By confidence, contribution,coping,control the situation

ᗡᗡᗡ

Emotional resilience works similarly. You're working out your 'resilience muscle' when you practice resilience, getting stronger daily.

ᗡᗡᗡ

By adapting some stress-releasing techniques to adjust to the situation

ᗡᗡᗡ

Pay attention to your health, mind your mindset, develop confidence

❧❧❧

By helping and by understanding.

❧❧❧

Practising relaxation techniques,

❧❧❧

Giving time for the students to talk to each other before starting or at the end of the period

❧❧❧

Having patience and confidence

ᚥᚥᚥ

Build my self-confidence. learn from my mistake and failure

ᚥᚥᚥ

By generating positive feelings and being open-minded and flexible. Talk to each other.

By meditation

ᚥᚥᚥ

By paying attention to our health, handling every situation effectively, setting our goals irrespective of their result, and having the attitude' I can do it.

Resilience is a critical strategy that helps employees tackle stress, a competitive job market, workplace conflicts, and challenges. Improving resilience is essential because employees identify work as the number one stressor in their lives.

Teach our students how to overcome fear and failure and treat feedback positively.

MANAGE STRESS, WORK WITH COLLEAGUES

I Practice thought awareness.

ᗞᗞᗞ

By working on different plans related to one issue and sometimes by ignoring something unnecessary.

ᗞᗞᗞ

Learning from mistakes Better Focus on physical wellness, relaxation techniques, connection, and self-awareness.

ᗞᗞᗞ

My inner strength and help from people around us.

ᗑᗑᗑ

By self-control, confidence and staying connected with others.

ᗑᗑᗑ

By being optimistic, having a positive relationship, confident and empathetic.

ᗑᗑᗑ

Self Awareness, patience, relaxed, positive mindset, work-life balance, and physical well-being.

ᗑᗑᗑ

Develop problem-solving skills.

ϸϸϸ

Pay Attention to your Health, Focus on your physical well-being, and Mind your mindset Practice self-awareness.

ϸϸϸ

Interactive, maintaining perspective, managing stress, building networks etc.

ϸϸϸ

By being a good listener, being a patient teacher, understanding the situation and then reacting. By managing the emotional aspects.

ʕʕʕ

By building confidence and by learning from the mistake.

ʕʕʕ

With a happiness quotient the first time every time.

ʕʕʕ

We can attain resilience at work by tackling stress and developing mental fitness.

ʕʕʕ

Resilience is the process and outcome of successfully adapting to complex or challenging life experiences.

ᗡᗡᗡ

Teaching students to set their goals, develop skills, lead them on overcoming emotional situations, etc.

ᗡᗡᗡ

Build your self-confidence by seeking advice.

ᗡᗡᗡ

बच्चो से बातचीत कर

ϸϸϸ

Mind your mindset.

ϸϸϸ

Resilience is the ability to bounce back from adversity.

ϸϸϸ

With keeping patience.

ϸϸϸ

By maintaining a healthy work-life balance.

ᘓᘓᘓ

By following the seven Cs', clarity, correctness, conciseness, courtesy, concreteness, consideration and completeness.

ᘓᘓᘓ

By positive thinking like I can, I will and by overcoming stress.

ᘓᘓᘓ

Pay attention to your health.

ᘓᘓᘓ

Focus on your physical well-being.

ɞɞɞ

Practice relaxation techniques.

ɞɞɞ

Practice reframing threats as challenges.

ɞɞɞ

Mind your mindset.

❧❧❧

Get connected.

❧❧❧

Practice self-awareness.

❧❧❧

Watch your stress levels.

❧❧❧

By practising self-awareness.

ﭬﭬﭬ

Pay attention to your health, focus on physical well-being, practice self-awareness, etc.

ﭬﭬﭬ

Resilience is a factor of mind and body. It should be encouraging to know that, as necessary as resilience is, many of the resilience factors that drive it are within our power to change.

ﭬﭬﭬ

Through Mentoring, with gratitude, believe in them, find the opportunity and help them.

ᘖᘖᘖ

Pay attention to your health.

ᘖᘖᘖ

Focus on your physical well-being.

ᘖᘖᘖ

Practice relaxation techniques.

ᘖᘖᘖ

Practice reframing threats as challenges.

ᐅᐅᐅ

Mind your mindset.

ᐅᐅᐅ

Get connected.

ᐅᐅᐅ

By reaching out to people, reflecting on past success, and believing in their abilities.

ᕯᕯᕯ

Patience as a hobby.

ᕯᕯᕯ

High tolerance of adverse effects as a practice.

ᕯᕯᕯ

By Drafting Personal goals.

ᕯᕯᕯ

Through the practice of a Stong sense of humour.

❧❧❧

By Adopting a High level of adaptability.

❧❧❧

Resilience is a critical strategy that helps employees tackle stress, a competitive job market, workplace conflicts, and challenges.

❧❧❧

Being Joyful at all times.

❧❧❧

Self-introspect and give time to ourselves.

ϷϷϷ

Taking things as a priority, recovering from setbacks, and practising self-awareness.

ϷϷϷ

By the conversation and clearing doubts.

ϷϷϷ

Explaining things and working for self.

ᢦᢦᢦ

Let us all cultivate a feeling of joy and togetherness at work.

ᢦᢦᢦ

Having patience.

ᢦᢦᢦ

Positive attitude, reflection, and recharge as one priorities.

ᢦᢦᢦ

Practice relaxation techniques, and self-awareness, Get Connected and Watch your stress level.

ϸϸϸ

By practising relaxation techniques with social cooperation.

ϸϸϸ

To help others develop new skills and instil a sense of purpose.

ϸϸϸ

Creating awareness and engaging with others, we can generate to overcome stress.

ᐅᐅᐅ

By striving forward and trying different things.

ᐅᐅᐅ

By Thinking positive.

ᐅᐅᐅ

They are challenging life experiences, primarily through mental, emotional, and behavioural flexibility and adjustment to external and internal demands.

ᐅᐅᐅ

By focusing on our physical well-being, watching our stress level, by practising self-awareness.

ᗩᗩᗩ

Through reflective analysis, one has to learn to Think positive. You can't always control life-changing events, but you can control how you respond to them.

ᗩᗩᗩ

By meditation, Building perspective, setting your goals and learning to relax.

ᗩᗩᗩ

Pay attention to our health and mindset, connect with people, and practice relaxation techniques.

ᐳᐳᐳ

By managing punctuality, We also attain resilience at work by - Paying attention to our health, Practicing reframing threats as challenges and Minding our mindset.

ᐳᐳᐳ

By being active through their involvement in studies.

ᐳᐳᐳ

Being patient and focused on the priorities. Developing hobbies and working on our inner self by engineering our thoughts and attitudes and, in the end, practising spirituality.

❥❥❥

*By talking to friends, Giving priority to work,
Continuously learning and Bouncing back out
of the trouble.*

❥❥❥

*By developing joyfulness at work and doing
Exercise, practising mindfulness.*

❥❥❥

Compartmentalise your cognitive load.

❥❥❥

Take detachment breaks.

ᛒᛒᛒ

Develop mental agility.

ᛒᛒᛒ

Cultivate compassion.

ᛒᛒᛒ

Adjusting with others.

ᛒᛒᛒ

By cultivating the feeling of joy and togetherness.

ᗞᗞᗞ

Pay attention to your health.

ᗞᗞᗞ

Through lots of efforts made by my coping, confidence, and contribution.

ᗞᗞᗞ

By developing patience.

ᕤᕤᕤ

Handling the situation intelligently and transparent mindset.

ᕤᕤᕤ

By training them.

ᕤᕤᕤ

By understanding its true meaning.

ᕤᕤᕤ

Pay attention to your health, practise relaxation techniques, get connected, watch your stress level and mind your mindset.

ᕣᕣᕣ

I keep myself in others' place and think about their views towards work. Or situation.

ᕣᕣᕣ

Pay attention to your health.

ᕣᕣᕣ

Focus on your physical well-being.

ᕣᕣᕣ

Practice relaxation techniques.

ᕗᕗᕗ

Practice reframing threats as challenges.

ᕗᕗᕗ

Mind your mindset.

ᕗᕗᕗ

Get connected.

ԂԂԂ

Practice self-awareness.

ԂԂԂ

Watch your stress levels.

ԂԂԂ

Mind your mindset, watch your stress level and practice relaxation techniques and Mindfulness.

ԂԂԂ

Patience and confidence.

ಶಿಶಿ

Gratitude, unique strength.

ಶಿಶಿ

To cultivate a feeling of joy and togetherness at work.

ಶಿಶಿ

Teaching and learning as a priority Very confidently In the classroom by cultivating a feeling of joy and togetherness and teaching the importance of health and well-being.

ϷϷϷ

Cooperating

Pay attention to your health. Mind your mindset.

ϷϷϷ

For knowledge

We can attain resilience at work -

By developing problem-solving skills.

ϷϷϷ

I am optimistic.

❦❦❦

Encouraging goal setting.

❦❦❦

We are maintaining a work-life balance.

❦❦❦

We are staying healthy.

❦❦❦

Proper sleep and exercise.

ᴆᴆᴆ

ManagingShe is managing stress.

ᴆᴆᴆ

RegulatingThey is regulating emotions.

ᴆᴆᴆ

*The building is building social networks/
relationships.*

ʖʖʖ

With a relaxed and calm nature, confidence.

ʖʖʖ

It helps employees tackle stress.

ʖʖʖ

By giving opportunities to students.

ʖʖʖ

A positive approach to work and outlook in life, in turn, enables better problem-solving and helps to maintain motivation.

᭢᭢᭢

By practising relaxation methods.

᭢᭢᭢

Flexibility in learning and exploring challenges.

᭢᭢᭢

Self Motivation and mediation.

᭢᭢᭢

I am feeling Joy and Togetherness at work.

ᛉᛉᛉ

Pay attention to your health.

ᛉᛉᛉ

Let us learn to cultivate a feeling of joy and togetherness at work and practice the self-awareness practice method to face challenges at work.

ᛉᛉᛉ

I persist with and focus on achieving objectives even in difficult circumstances.

ᐅᐅᐅ

I remain optimistic.

ᐅᐅᐅ

We are monitoring our emotional reactions and remaining controlled.

ᐅᐅᐅ

By keeping patience.

ᐅᐅᐅ

I am learning to relax, burst stress, treat problems and failures as a learning process, and emerge as a winner.

ϷϷϷ

A healthy mind, teamwork Paying attention to our health and practising relaxation techniques build our mindset, connect, and practice self-awareness by not giving up and reflective analysis of failure.

ϷϷϷ

To make our work more effective.

Managing emotions and stressful situations by 7cs

For development. viz. clarity, correctness, conciseness, courtesy, concreteness, consideration and completeness.

❧❧❧

Cherish social support and interaction. Good relationships with family and friends, and others are vital. Being active in the broader community also helps.

❧❧❧

Mind your mindset and Pay attention to your health. Practice relaxation techniques to manage stress, get connected, mind your mindset and be flexible.

❧❧❧

Pay attention to your health.
Focus on your physical well-being.
Practice relaxation techniques.
Practice reframing threats as challenges.
Mind your mindset.

ᗞᗞᗞ

By focusing on physical well-being.

I am practising relaxation techniques.

ᗞᗞᗞ

By practising self-awareness.

ᗞᗞᗞ

Resilience is a critical strategy that helps employees tackle stress, a competitive job market, and workplace conflicts and address challenges on the job.

ᗺᗺᗺ

We are developing self-confidence.

Practice relaxation techniques and self-awareness and get connected.

To handle the tuff situation.

ᗺᗺᗺ

By getting connected, being self-aware, controlling stress levels, minding our mindset and being healthy.

ϸϸϸ

By being confident and persevering.

ϸϸϸ

Label difficult emotions.

ϸϸϸ

By adopting Flexibility and adaptability.

ϸϸϸ

Through mediation.

ᕔᕔᕔ

Very confidently.

ᕔᕔᕔ

BY BEING FOCUSED ON WORK. MIND MY MINDSET.

ᕔᕔᕔ

By enjoying doing that work and feeling togetherness.

ᕔᕔᕔ

Practising flexibility.

ppp

By not stressing and taking things as it comes. Finding ways to overcome it and find other options.

ppp

Think positive, look after yourself, use your support network, work towards a goal and seek help.

ppp

We can attain resilience at work by working together with a feeling of joy and happiness.

ϸϸϸ

Togetherness and feeling of joy at work.

ϸϸϸ

Relax, be aware, Edit your outlook, learn from your mistakes and failures, set goals, and be confident.

ϸϸϸ

Learn to be flexible and cultivate a feeling of joy and togetherness at work.

ϸϸϸ

Be patient and time management. Pay attention to our health.

ԾԾԾ

Promoting positive emotions fosters a sense of competence, encourages goal setting, and develops problem-solving skills.

ԾԾԾ

Resilience is a critical strategy that helps employees tackle stress, a competitive job market, and workplace conflicts and address challenges on the job.

ԾԾԾ

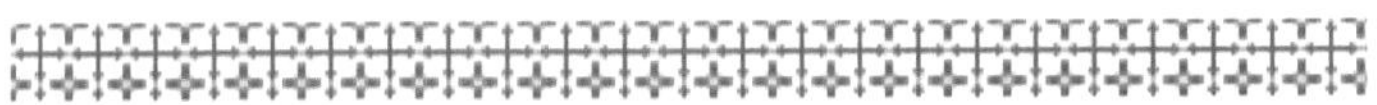

Improving resilience is essential because employees identify work as the number one stressor in their lives.

❥❥❥

Make every day everyday meaningful, positive relationships with all persons in the workplace daily meaningful, positive relationship with all persons in the workplace every day.

❥❥❥

PAY ATTENTION TO HEALTH GOOD MINDSET

❥❥❥

*Pay attention to your health. Focus on your
physical being.
Mind your mindset.*

❦❦❦

*By addressing the challenges, and practising
patience,*

*let us all cultivate a feeling joyful and
togetherness.*

❦❦❦

*Working together By enabling a feeling of Joy
and togetherness at work.*

❦❦❦

By developing a sense of joy and togetherness at work.

ppp

Cultivate a feeling of joy and togetherness at work.

ppp

Focus on our physical well-being, and practice relaxation techniques.

ppp

Many activities like instruments help to attain resilience during a career.

ppp

Focus on your physical well-being and practice self-awareness.

❧❧❧

Practice relaxation techniques, reframe threats as challenges, and Mind your mindset. Practice self-awareness, and Watch your stress levels.

❧❧❧

By taking active participation.

❧❧❧

Practice relaxation techniques.

ೞೞೞ

By creating a supportive atmosphere celebrating the success of students in class.

ೞೞೞ

By having positive energy.

ೞೞೞ

Continuous work and corrective introspection.

ೞೞೞ

By keeping the mind calm and not taking stress.

❥❥❥

Practice reframing threats as challenges.
Mind your mindset.
Get connected.

❥❥❥

Remaining optimistic.

❥❥❥

To give a chance to every student.

ᐅᐅᐅ

Seeking help and framing a positive outlook.

ᐅᐅᐅ

Overcome obstacles, Bounce back from perceived failure.

ᐅᐅᐅ

Take things as they come, can overcome hardships, and develop confidence.

ᐅᐅᐅ

By cultivating a feeling of joy and togetherness at work.

Get Connected By doing hard work.

Togetherness.

ᐅᐅᐅ

We are focusing on work and taking care of our health. Taking care of our mental stress level. etc

ᐅᐅᐅ

Giving time to ourselves and understanding the whole process.

ᐅᐅᐅ

By planning my work systematic and straightforward.

ᴘᴘᴘ

By giving assignments on each topic in the classroom.

ᴘᴘᴘ

Develop mental agility, Cultivate compassion, Compartmentalize your cognitive load, Exercise mindfulness, Think positive, and Work towards a goal.

ᴘᴘᴘ

By being together and creating a joyful situation.

ᑭᑭᑭ

By planning our work systematically.

ᑭᑭᑭ

With continuous effort and staying positive, set goals and make strong relationships.

ᑭᑭᑭ

The plan for that particular day was to be confident in our work.

ᑭᑭᑭ

By gaining confidence, control and peace.

ﭢﭢﭢ

Resilience can be attained if we work as a team, accept our mistakes, and try to correct them. It helps in developing tolerance as well.

ﭢﭢﭢ

By focusing, On determination, dedication and sincerity.

ﭢﭢﭢ

Cherish social support and interaction. Good relationships with family and friends, and others are vital. Being active in the broader community also helps.
Treat problems as a learning process. Develop the habit of using challenges as opportunities to acquire or master skills and build achievement.

ÞÞÞ

Helping others and contributing to the community helps develop and attain resilience at work.

ÞÞÞ

Developing students, Supporting colleagues' mental health, Developing new skills, Being attentive and above all, Paying attention.

❧❧❧

By practising self-awareness and having a consistently positive outlook.

❧❧❧

Deal with each difficult situation they face with ease.

❧❧❧

Don't exhibit excessive negative emotions

during difficult times.

ᛩᛩᛩ

Practice relaxation techniques.

ᛩᛩᛩ

Practice self-awareness,
Watch mental and physical health and get rid
of stress.

ᛩᛩᛩ

By cooperating with others.

ᛩᛩᛩ

Resilience is a crucial critical strategy that helps employees tackle stress, a competitive job market, and workplace conflicts and address challenges on the job.

ppp

With an incredible relaxed and calm nature and confidence.

ppp

Model learning from mistakes.

ppp

Encourage responsible risks and Label difficult emotions.

ᐅᐅᐅ

Write and talk about setbacks and human resilience.

ᐅᐅᐅ

Be calm and do work clearly.

ᐅᐅᐅ

Enthusiasm, commitment along with a positive outlook for students.

❧❧❧

Giving them different tasks through brilliant ways and Balanced emotions.

❧❧❧

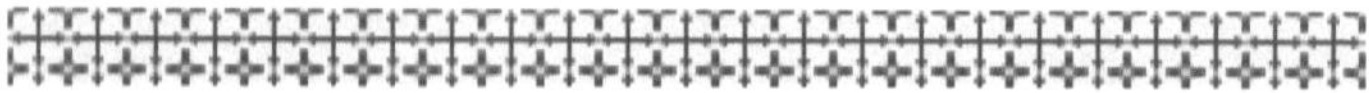

People should be aware of their physical and mental health while dealing with stress. They must practice relaxing exercises and calm their mind with activities they love to do once in a while.

❧❧❧

Attention to health. Get connected to people. Bounce back.

ᚱᚱᚱ

Focus on physical well-being, relaxation techniques, get related, and practise self-awareness.

ᚱᚱᚱ

Be authentic, Maintain perspective, Manage stress, Work with your colleagues, and stay healthy.

ᚱᚱᚱ

Positively take criticism, complain, be flexible with situations, and move forward in all cases.

ϷϷϷ

By doing work on time. Be authentic, Maintain perspective, Manage stress, Work with your colleagues, and stay healthy.

ϷϷϷ

Through Interacting, Cooperating, Managing Emotions, and portraying Good character.

ϷϷϷ

By making the practice of relaxation techniques focus on physical well-being, practising self-awareness, Practising resilience techniques and Supporting each other if working in a team.

❦❦❦

Practice resilience techniques Attain them with effect

Peace is the spectrum of learning, catering to the situation.

❦❦❦

Having a realistic sense of control over one's choices. Understanding the limitations of such power, Seeing change as an opportunity or challenge
Secure attachments with others and the ability to engage their support.

❦❦❦

Personal goals, Strong sense of humour, Patience, High tolerance for negative affect An optimistic outlook and a High level of adaptability.

ᖰᖰᖰ

Through meditation, By keeping calm.

ᖰᖰᖰ

By setting goals, thinking positive and staying determined by incorporating Positive and reactive skills.

ᖰᖰᖰ

Think positively, work together with others, seek help

Relaxing, focusing, and connecting with people reduce stress levels, Will power with a positive attitude.

ᏠᏠᏠ

Set your goal. Watch your stress level. Focus on your health. Be connected.

ᏠᏠᏠ

Pay attention to your health, and Focus on your sound - being well-being. Practise relaxation techniques.

ϷϷϷ

Being resilient gives them the ability to tackle this head-on, bounce back from setbacks and have the best chance of succeeding. It allows them to learn and grow in all situations – two skills crucial to well-being and development.

ϷϷϷ

By having a positive attitude - I can and will cooperate with others, and By keeping myself calm.

ϷϷϷ

Practice relaxation
Focus on physical well-being.

ϷϷϷ

Learning it again and redoing it until
successfully achieving the goals.

ϷϷϷ

Health should be taken care of so that we can
think in a positive direction. We must have a
healthy mindset. We should take our threats as
our challenges. We should practice self-
awareness. We must watch our stress levels.

ϷϷϷ

I persist with and focus on achieving objectives even in difficult circumstances.
I remain optimistic.
We are monitoring our emotional reactions and remaining controlled.

ÞÞÞ

Practice reframing threats as challenges. To attain resilience at work with self-confidence by emerging muscular flexibility and promoting gratitude.

ÞÞÞ

Practice self-awareness and knowledge sharing through positive conversations, group discussions, paying attention, focusing, relaxing your mind, getting connected, minding your mindset, etc.

ÞÞÞ

Resilience is a critical strategy that helps employees tackle stress, a competitive job market, and workplace conflicts and address challenges on the job. Improving resilience is essential because employees identify work as the number one stressor in their lives.

ᐅᐅᐅ

By cultivating a feeling of joy and togetherness at work.

ᐅᐅᐅ

By paying attention to our health, focusing on physical well-being, by self-awareness and

Developing new skills.

❧❧❧

Understand the difficulties and find ways to overcome them.

❧❧❧

By improving adaptability and flexibility, self-compassion, and cognitive agility.

❧❧❧

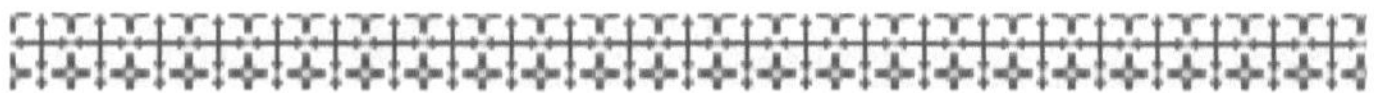

Resilience in the workplace can help people recover from challenging experiences. It can also assist their growth and development.

❧❧❧

By cultivating a feeling of joy and togetherness at work.

❧❧❧

By being updated with the changes and understanding.

❧❧❧

Thinking strategically.

❧❧❧

By focusing on students' physical well-being.

ppp

By being flexible and open-minded
Generate positive feelings
Be realistically optimistic
By using unique strength
Maintain perspective.

ppp

We can attain resilience through mentoring and talking with each other, encouraging us to keep up the good work and promoting gratitude.

ᐅᐅᐅ

Dr Ginsburg, a child paediatrician and human development expert, proposes that seven integral and interrelated components make up resilience – competence, confidence, connection, character, contribution, coping and control.

ᐅᐅᐅ

Focus on physical well-being, practice self-awareness, and get connected.

By cultivating a feeling of joy and togetherness at work.

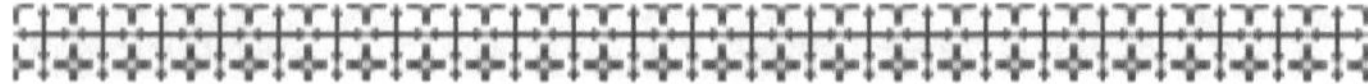

By setting some goals.

Resilient people experience stress, setbacks, and complicated emotions, but they tap into their strengths and seek help from support systems to overcome challenges and work through problems. Resilience empowers them to accept and adapt to a situation and move forward.

ᐳᐳᐳ

Get connected, practice self-awareness, and practice relaxation techniques.

ᐳᐳᐳ

Resilience in the workplace can help people recover from challenging experiences. It can also assist their growth and development.

ᗑᗑᗑ

With polite behaviour and trying to understand everyone's emotions.

ᗑᗑᗑ

Develop new skills and encapsulate Mentoring and talking with each other encourages us to keep up the excellent work and promotes gratitude.

ᗑᗑᗑ

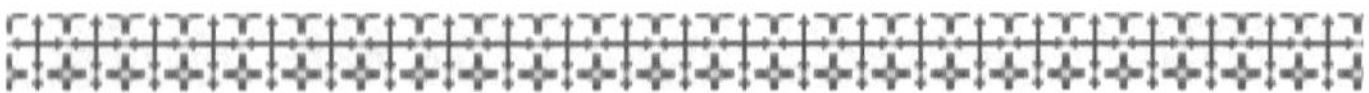

Resilience can help employees manage stress and motivate them to face challenges with determination.

ᑭᑭᑭ

By continuously strengthening one's abilities and brushing up on working skills.

ᑭᑭᑭ

In positive workplace relationships, resilient workers will do what they can to help another

person succeed.

ᗡᗡᗡ

Practice more relaxation techniques.

Resilience enables a positive approach to work and outlook on life, which in turn enables better problem-solving and helps to maintain motivation.

Conclusion:

Encourage children to see things from the points of view of a variety of different people and groups. This involves having a respectful attitude toward people's many differences, such as colour, religion, sexual orientation, age, emotions, aptitude levels, and other distinctions among individuals, as well as an awareness of how these distinctions might expand ways of thinking and doing.

Resilience may drive forward progress. Assist youngsters in developing the skills necessary to face and prevail over adversity and uncertainty by assisting them in conceiving of and putting into action novel and concerted methods that make challenging circumstances bearable and achieving success in conquering obstacles.

About The Author

Dheeraj Mehrotra, MS, MPhil, PhD (Education Management) honoris causa., a white and a yellow belt in SIX SIGMA, a Certified NLP Business Diploma holder, is an Educational Innovator, Author, with expertise in Six Sigma In Education, Academic Audits, Neuro-Linguistic Programming (NLP), Total Quality Management In Education, an Experiential Educator, a CBSE Resource towards School Assessment (SQAA), CCE, JIT, Five S, and KAIZEN. He has authored over 100 books on topics which include Computer Science, AI, Digital Body Language, NLP, Quality Circles, School Management, Classroom Effectiveness and Safety and security in schools. A former Principal at De Indian Public School, New Delhi, (INDIA), NPS International School, Guwahati, and Education Officer at GEMS, Gurgaon, with an ample teaching experience of over Two Decades, he is a certified Trainer for Quality Circles/ TQM in Education and QCI Standards for School Accreditation/ School Audits and Management. He has also been honoured with the President of India's National Teacher Award in the year 2006 and the Best Science Teacher State Award (By the Ministry of Science and Technology, State of UP), Innovation in Education for his inception of Six Sigma In Education by Education Watch, New Delhi and Education World- Best Teacher Award, BOLT Learner Teacher Award by Air India, 'Innovation in Education Award 2016' by Higher Education Forum (HEF), Gujarat Chapter, among others. He has developed over 150 FREE EDUCATIONAL MOBILE Apps for the Google Play Store exclusively for Teachers, Students, and Parents. This work has been recognised by the LIMCA

BOOK OF RECORDS & INDIA BOOK OF RECORDS as the only Indian to draw that feast. Dr Mehrotra works as a PRINCIPAL at KUNWARS GLOBAL SCHOOL, Lucknow, in India. He has conducted over 1000 workshops globally on "Excellence In Education" integrated with Total Quality Management and Six Sigma, Technology Integration in Education (TIE), Developing towards being ROCKSTAR TEACHERS, including Cyberspace, Cyber Security, Classroom Management, School Leadership & Management, and Innovative teaching within classrooms via Mind Maps, NLP and Experiential Learning in Academics. He is an active TEDx speaker and can be viewed on the youtube TEDx channel.

As a premium UDEMY Instructor, he has developed over 450 courses and caters to over 8 Lakh students from 180 countries.

He can be visited at www.authordheerajmehrotra.com.

Books By The Same Author